Two legged leap

Triple twist take-off

For Helen English – E.V.T.

For Seren, Christie & Lucy – H.E.B.

FELICITY WISHES
Written by Emma Thomson and Helen Bailey
Illustrated by Emma Thomson

A catalogue record of this book is available from the British Library.
ISBN 0 340 84400 0 (PB)
Felicity Wishes © 2000 Emma Thomson. Licensed by White Lion Publishing.
Felicity Wishes: Friendship and Fairyschool © 2001 Emma Thomson.

The right of Emma Thomson and Helen Bailey to be identified as the authors
and Emma Thomson as the illustrator of this Work has been asserted by
WLP in accordance with the Copyright, Designs and Patents Act 1988.

First PB edition published 2002
4 6 8 10 9 7 5 3

Published by Hodder Children's Books, a division of Hodder Headline Limited,
338 Euston Road, London, NW1 3BH

Printed in China

Emma Thomson's
felicity Wishes

Friendship and Fairyschool

Hodder
Children's
Books

A division of Hodder Headline Limited

Felicity Wishes was looking forward to the first day of her last term at the School of Nine Wishes. She'd spent ages choosing what to wear and had finally settled on a pink dress. She almost always chose pink as it was her favourite colour.

She had her new pink pencil case,

a new pink school bag,

and a brand new pink diary to
keep all her secrets and wishes safe.

The only thing left to decide was what
kind of fairy she wanted to be!

When Felicity arrived, all her friends were fluttering around the school gates, gossiping and giggling. 'I can't believe this is our last term, ever!' said Felicity's best friend, Polly.

'I can't believe I don't know
what I want to do when I finish
school!' said Felicity nervously.

Poor Felicity! School hadn't always been a great success.
Her maths didn't add up.

She was
behind in
history.

She didn't know where she was in geography...

. . .and science never went according to plan!

It seemed everyone was good at something.
Except Felicity.
It seemed everyone knew what kind
of fairy she wanted to be.
Except Felicity.

Polly
wanted to be
a Tooth Fairy. She knew
how to get from America
to China via Africa, except
she couldn't fly and hold
her wand, the coins and
teeth all at the
same time. She
kept veering off course.

TOOTH
BAG

So, in
sewing class, Felicity
made Polly a little bag
to carry everything.

Daisy longed to be a Blossom Fairy.

She loved growing things, but in gardening class . . . Atishoo!
Daisy sneezed so hard her crown fell off.
Atishoo! Daisy sneezed even harder.
Atishoo! She sneezed so
hard she blew all the petals
off her beautiful rose.
'Whoever heard of a Blossom Fairy
with hay fever?' sniffed Daisy sadly.

Felicity gave her a special handkerchief
filled with magic dust
to use next time Daisy sneezed.

Magical Fairy Handkerchief

with added sparkle!

As soon as she felt her nose twitch, Daisy
clamped the handkerchief to her face and,
magically, the sneeze disappeared.

Holly (who was a little lazy) dreamed of being
the Fairy on the Christmas tree.
'It isn't a full-time job and there's hardly any
flying involved,' she told Felicity, 'so if it wasn't
for one small problem, I'd be ideally suited.'
'What small problem?'
'I'm scared of heights,' confessed Holly.

'Holly you'd make a perfect Christmas Fairy,'
said Felicity encouragingly. 'You could start with
a small tree. Just imagine: the lights, the tinsel,
watching all the Christmas fun. Everyone looks
up to the fairy on the Christmas tree!'
'You know,' said Holly, her confidence growing,
'I think I could do it, in fact, I know I could!'

All term Felicity tried as hard as she
could but she still did not know
what kind of fairy she really wanted to be.
In cookery, she baked a cake so light it floated
away and no one could catch it.

In flying, she tried a triple twist take-off and sprained her wing.

In science, her sparkle dust mixture had the whole class sparkling – all week!
And, in history, she spent more time admiring her pink handwriting than finishing her project.

At last it was
time for Fairy Prize Day
when all the fairies leaving
school would be given their
tasks and a brand
new pair of beautiful,
sparkling wings.

Fairy Godmother
addressed the school:
'The task of Tooth Fairy
goes to . . .

The delicate task of
Blossom Fairy goes to . . .
Daisy!

The special task of
Christmas Fairy goes to . . .
Holly!

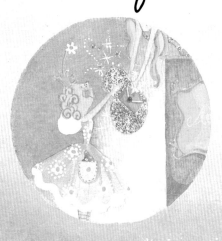

Fairy Godmother put down her notes, and said, 'There is one fairy who has helped her friends achieve their dreams. This special fairy deserves the most important title of all.

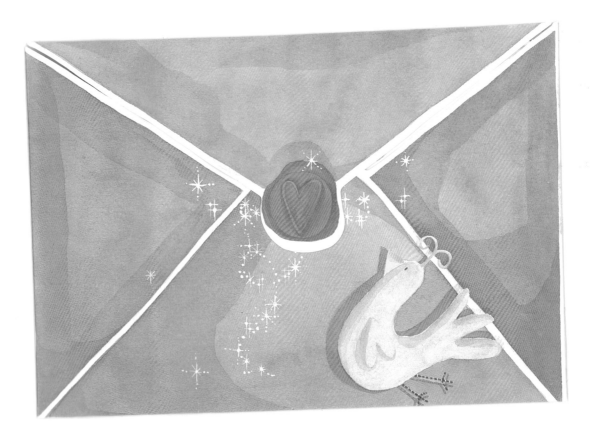

The award of Friendship Fairy goes to . . .

Felicity was so surprised her
cheeks went as pink as her dress.
She floated up to the stage and there,
waiting to make her a proper fairy, was the biggest,
brightest pair of sparkly wings she had ever seen.

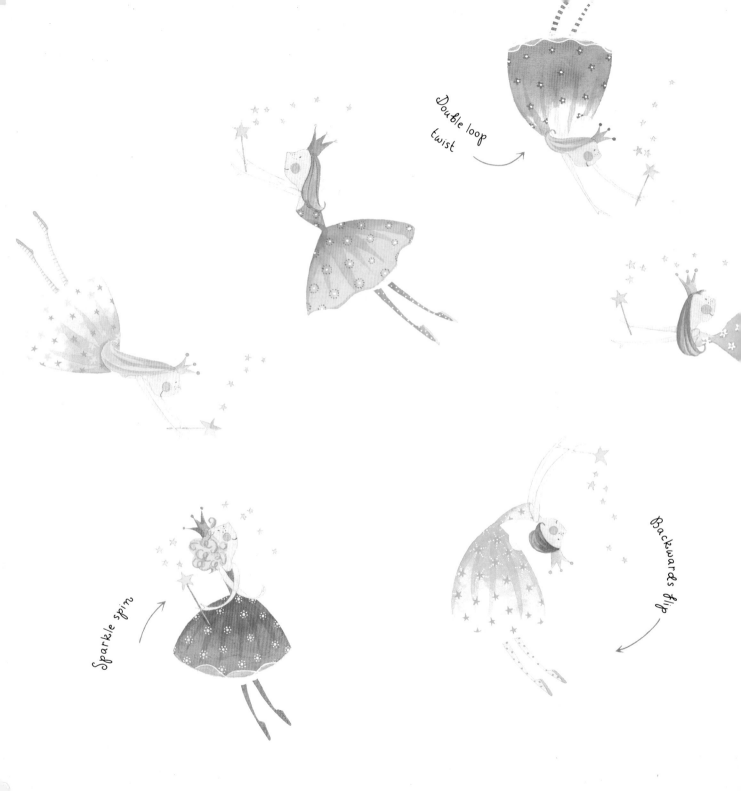

Double loop
twist

Backwards flip

Sparkle spin